F is for
Fierce Female Founders

by Rachel Neill

First Edition: November 2020
Printed in the United States of America: November 2020
ISBN: 9780578785455

To Pippa - my little love who will move mountains.

Girls can do anything, not just climb to the top but build it from the ground up. When you think about the things you want to do, let these fierce female founders inspire.

A is for **Arianna Huffington**
who's boldly building a media empire.

HuffPost

B is for **Brit Morin**

bringing DIY – do it yourself - into our lives,
making us laugh along the way!

Brit + CO

C is for **Charlee Moore**

making heaps of healthy food for everyone.

Bob's Red Mill

D is for **Debbie Fields**

who deliciously dominates the sweet treat industry.

Mrs. Fields Cookies

E is for Emily Weiss

disrupting the beauty industry with a dazzling success!

Glossier

F is for **Feyi Olopade Ayodele**
a fierce female founder, helping battle cancer.

G is for Gail Liniger

a real estate mogul – a powerful person –
heralding homes to people in every state.

FOR SALE

Re/Max Holdings

H is for Holly Thaggard

pushing to protect our largest organ - our skin - from the sun.

SuperGoop

I is for ILANA NANKIN

who teaches us to breathe, bend, and be bold.

Breathe For Change

J is for **Judy Faulkner**

the goddess of health tech.

Epic

K is for Katie Rodan and Kathy Fields

sending us spa-worthy skincare products.

Rodan & Fields

L is for Lisa Skeete Tatum

creating an awesome app to boost the strength of women in the workplace.

Landit

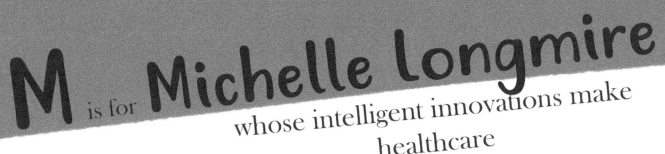

M is for Michelle Longmire

whose intelligent innovations make healthcare better for everyone.

Medable

N is for **Nora Khaldi**

unlocking biotechnological secrets to help our health.

Nuritas

R is for **Rachel Neill**

entrepreneur with a love for starting new companies, supporting female founders, and, of course, writing books!

S is for **Sara Blakely**

gloriously glamorizing our undergarments.

Spanx

T is for **Tina Sharkey**

who shows the value of removing labels all while being exceedingly eco-friendly.

Brandless

U is for **Uma Raghavan**

who developed a superb software for companies
to manage personal info and state rules!

Integris Software

V is for Vera Wang

who wows us with fun and fabulous fashion!

Vera Wang

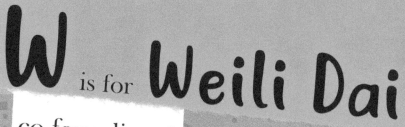

W is for **Weili Dai**

co-founding the company that creates seriously cool semiconductors.

Marvell Technologies

X is for Xiaoyin Qu

pulling people together virtually across the globe!

Run The World

Y is for **Yuhna Kim**

who makes marvelous meditation tech for anyone
who wants to 'Om'!

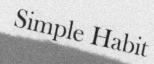

Simple Habit

Z is for Zawadi Byant

making sure your parents can take you to a doctor if you're super sick at night.

Nightlight Pediatric Urgent Care

Fierce Female Founders

Girls can do anything

CPSIA information can be obtained
at www.ICGtesting.com
Printed in the USA
BVHW021958030921
615981BV00006B/522

9 780578 785455